Why Do
We Baptize
Infants?

Basics of the Faith

Sean Michael Lucas, Series Editor

Why Do We Baptize Infants?

BRYAN CHAPELL

P&R
PUBLISHING
P.O. BOX 817 • PHILLIPSBURG • NEW JERSEY 08865-0817

Page Design by Tobias Design

Printed in the United States of America

Library of Congress Control Number: 2006934631

ISBN-13: 978-1-59638-058-5

■ **Why do Presbyterians baptize infants?** We must confess that some bring their children for this sacrament because of the sweetness of the ceremony, or because of the traditions of family and church, or even with the misguided expectation that somehow "holy water" will magically protect their child from hell. Yet neither sentiment nor tradition nor superstition is sufficient reason for believers to bring their children to be baptized. And, thankfully, such reasons are not the basis of our church's practice. We baptize infants because we believe that the Bible teaches us to do so.

My goal in this booklet is to explain pastorally the scriptural foundation for infant baptism. To do this, I will first present the biblical support for infant baptism as I have presented it in new members' and church officers' training classes over the past twenty-five years. Then I will conclude by offering words of explanation that I have often used as a pastor during the administration of the ordinance. My goals are to help explain why we should baptize the infants of believing parents and also to help pastors better know how to administer the sacrament in ways that are meaningful and helpful for their churches. Thus, I plan to present this material in terms that are accessible to laypersons, leaving technical discussions to able scholars in other books.

One further word of preparation relates to my own journey regarding baptism. I did not always accept the practice of infant baptism. I was raised among dedicated, faithful, and well-instructed Baptists who believed that the Bible regards only those who decide to follow Christ as proper candidates for baptism. As a result, I well understand and respect those who have questions about the legitimacy of a practice that they feel has no biblical warrant. I also do not want to do or teach anything that the Bible does not support. Thus, the paragraphs that follow are more than the recitation of a party line; they are the reflection of the thought process that led me to believe that Scripture teaches that God wants believing parents to present their children to him in baptism.

The biblical explanation will flow as follows:

I. The Biblical Background of Infant Baptism
 Salvation is through the *covenant of faith* in the Old
  and New Testaments.
 The faithful receive a *covenant sign* in the Old Testament.
 The *covenant continues* in the New Testament.
 The *covenant sign changes* to reflect New Testament
  blessings.
II. The Biblical Basis for Infant Baptism
 The absence of a contrary command
 The examples of household baptism
III. The Biblical Benefits of Infant Baptism
 The devotion of parents
 The blessing of children

THE BIBLICAL BACKGROUND OF INFANT BAPTISM

The Covenant of Faith
 Many of the children in our churches enjoy singing the song "Father Abraham Had Many Sons." This song contains a

vital New Testament truth: "Father Abraham had many sons— I am one of them and so are you." When they sing these words, our children are not merely echoing a statement of faith that a Jewish child in the Old Testament could make. The truth of these words *still* applies.

A key concept in the New Testament is that *all* of God's people (Jew or Gentile—past or present) are blessed in accordance with the covenant (i.e., promise of blessing) that God made with Abraham. The Lord promised in this "everlasting covenant" that Abraham and his descendants would know God's blessings on the basis of faith in his provision (Gen. 15:1–6; 17:1–8). No one was to receive God's blessings on the basis of personal merit or on the basis of some ceremony. Out of his mercy alone—and before they could qualify for it in any way—the Lord covenanted to be the God of Abraham and his descendants (Gen. 17:7). The people would know and claim the blessings of this covenant by expressing faith in God's provision as Abraham had done (Gen. 15:6). Thus, God promised always to bless Abraham and his descendants by grace through faith (cf. Eph. 2:8–9).

But what does a covenant with a Jewish patriarch have to do with people in God's church today? The apostle Paul reminds us that God said to Abraham, "All nations will be blessed through you" (Gal. 3:8; cf. Gen. 12:3). The "everlasting covenant" that God made with Abraham (Gen. 17:7) continues to be in effect and continues to cover us. The Apostle Paul writes, "So those who have faith are blessed along with Abraham, the man of faith" (Gal. 3:9).

This means that we who have faith in Christ as God's provision for our salvation are blessed in accordance with Abraham's covenant. We are Abraham's spiritual descendants and are still covered by the covenant that God first made with him. Paul writes, "Consider Abraham: 'He believed God, and it was credited to him as righteousness.' Understand, then, that those who believe are children of Abraham" (Gal. 3:6–7). Whether or not they are biological descendants of Abraham, believers today are his spiritual children through the everlasting covenant that God provided through Abraham.

There is no other way to be a child of God than to be included in Abraham's covenant. There is no other covenant of salvation, and unless we are part of Abraham's covenant, we are not part of God's people. As the apostle says, "He [Christ] redeemed us in order that the blessing given to Abraham might come to the Gentiles through Christ Jesus" (Gal. 3:14). Those who have faith in Jesus Christ as their Savior receive the covenant promises of Abraham and are his spiritual children, regardless of their time or place of birth (cf. Gal. 3:29).

The Covenant Sign

After making the covenant with Abraham to bless him and his descendants by grace through faith, God provided a covenant sign both to mark those who were recipients of his promise and to signify his pledge to provide for those who had faith in him. It is important to remember that the sign was given after the covenant had already been made; it was neither a precondition of the covenant nor a means of manufacturing it. Faith was and is the sole condition of knowing the blessings of God's covenant.

The sign of circumcision. The covenant sign that God gave the Old Testament people was circumcision. The removal of the foreskin from the male reproductive organ signified the removal of spiritual uncleanness from God's people and communicated that God's provision for blessing was being passed on to all the children of Abraham from generation to generation (cf. Gen. 17:10–14; Deut. 10:16; Jer. 4:4; Col. 2:13).

Circumcision marked God's people as being separated and consecrated unto him and, consequently, as being in union with him and with each other in covenant-family and community relationships (Ex. 12:48; Deut. 30:6; Jer. 4:4; 9:26). The rite of circumcision necessarily involved the shedding of blood, and was one of numerous Old Testament signs that prefigured the blood that would be required of Christ in order for our sins to be removed (cf. Heb. 9:22).

The extent of the sign. Because God's promises extended to Abraham's house, *he was to devote all that he had to the Lord and to show it* by use of the covenant sign. This meant that all who were part of Abraham's household in that ancient society were to be devoted to God by the sign of circumcision—sons, dependent relatives, and servants (Gen. 17:23; cf. Ex. 12:43–48). In contemporary culture, we are not as accustomed to thinking of the head of a household as deciding the spiritual commitments of all its dependent members. However, the biblical perspective is that the head of the household represents the family to God and commits them to his worship. The representative role of heads of households has great scriptural precedent and rich implications in both the Old and the New Testaments (cf. Eph. 5:25–27; Heb. 11:7).

The representative principle helps to explain why Abraham devoted all in his house to God through the use of the Old Testament covenant sign, even though some of its members would not yet have expressed their faith. Abraham recognized his need as the head of a household to honor the Lord's promise to be the God of him and his family. The representative principle also explains why, in the New Testament, the apostle Paul could still say that children of a believing parent—even one who is married to a nonbeliever—are "holy" before God (1 Cor. 7:14). Few verses in Scripture more forcefully indicate that God communicates his grace to children while they are in the household of a covenant parent. Scripture does not contend that an adult who has turned from a parent's faith can presume to receive the eternal salvation promised through Abraham's covenant, but while children remain under the authority of a believing parent, they are covenantally represented by that parent's faith.

The principle of representation by the head of the household also explains why the practice of circumcision was not an indication that women were excluded from the covenant. Both through the act of procreation and through the representative principle implied by circumcision, the rite showed that the covenant promises were extended to all in the house regardless of descent or gender. An adopted child of either gender or even a dependent servant had equal spiritual standing with a biological son through the representative principle that circumcision signified. The ancient people were slow to realize these spiritual implications, but the New Testament drives the meaning home:

> You are all sons of God through faith in Christ Jesus. . . . There is neither Jew nor Greek, slave nor free, male nor female, for you are all one in Christ Jesus. If you belong to Christ, then you are Abraham's seed, and heirs according to the promise. (Gal. 3:26–29)

The relationship between sign and seal. We must still answer the question why the covenant sign was administered to those who had not yet expressed faith in God's provision. Since the covenant was made to express God's blessings to those who placed their faith in him, and since the covenant could be experienced only through faith, why did God tell Abraham to circumcise all the males in his household even before they knew of God's covenant of faith? Even if all of Abraham's house could have heard of God's provision and placed their faith in the Lord, no one would expect all of Abraham's descendants to put their faith in God by the time they were eight days old and required to be circumcised (Gen. 17:12). Why, then, was the covenant sign commanded for all?

The answer to why those who were saved through faith alone were still allowed to be circumcised as children (i.e., before they were able to express their faith) has important implications for administering the covenant sign to infants today. Does the requirement of faith for salvation preclude the possibility of administering a covenant sign to the children of believers? It did not in the Old Testament practice of circumcision, and the New Testament tells us why. The apostle Paul says in the book of Romans that circumcision was a "seal" as well as a "sign" of the righteousness that Abraham had by faith (Rom. 4:11). Both terms have important significance for our understanding of the application of covenant sacraments.

We can easily understand how circumcision was a "sign" of the righteousness provided through God's covenant. The putting off of uncleanness by the shedding of blood and the marking of the faithful as God's special people resonate with many familiar New Testament concepts. But the concept of a "seal" is less familiar to us today.

The "seal" image that the apostle calls to mind is that of the wax affixed to a letter or document and marked with a signet ring (or other instrument) to authenticate the source and validity of the document's contents. The seal acted as a visible pledge by the author to honor what he had covenanted to do in the document when the conditions it described were met. Circumcision was God's way of marking his people with a visible pledge to honor his covenant for those who expressed faith in him. Just as a seal is the pledge of its author that he will uphold his promises when described conditions are met, so circumcision was God's pledge to provide all the blessings of his covenant when the condition of faith was met. Our faith does not create God's covenant or cause it to be extended to us—he chose us in Christ before the foundation of the world (Eph. 1:4)—but our faith does claim (and live out) the covenant blessings that God provides by his grace and pledges with his seal.

A seal's validity does not depend on the time that the conditions of the covenant accompanying it are met. Like the seal of a document, the seal of circumcision could be applied long before recipients of promised and signified blessings met the conditions of the covenant. The seal was simply *the visible pledge of God that when the conditions of his covenant were met, the blessings he had promised would apply* (cf. Westminster Confession of Faith XXVIII.6). For this reason, God did not require that covenant parents wait until a child could express faith before commanding them to administer the covenant sign and seal of circumcision.

The Covenant Continuation

The New Testament apostles and writers take much care to let us know that the principles of the covenant of faith remain in effect for us (Luke 1:68–75; Acts 3:25). When Peter preaches on the day of Pentecost, he says to his thousands of Jewish listeners, "Repent and be baptized, every one of you, in the name of Jesus Christ for the forgiveness of your sins. . . . The promise is for you and your children and for all who are far off—for all whom the Lord our God will call" (Acts 2:38–39). Peter frames his call to salvation in Christ in covenantal terms by speaking of a promise that applies to his listeners and to their children as well as to others who are yet far off. The apostle assumes that God continues to relate to us as individuals and as families—that the covenant principles are still in effect. Individuals (even in covenant families) are still responsible to express their personal faith, but God continues to work out his gracious promises in families as well as extending the covenant to others.

The apostle Paul is more explicit about the continuation of the Abrahamic covenant and proclaims, "Those who believe are children of Abraham" (Gal. 3:7). He goes on to say that the law of Moses "does not set aside the covenant previously established by God and thus do away with the promise. . . . If you belong to Christ, then you are Abraham's seed, and heirs according to the promise" (Gal. 3:17, 29).

God's promise to Abraham to save those who have faith in heaven's provision remains in effect. Never do any come to God on the basis of their merit or because they have participated in some ritual. *Both the Old Testament and the New affirm God's continuing covenant promise to Abraham to bless people by divine grace through faith.*

The Change in the Covenant Sign

While the covenant continues, its sign changes to reflect what God has done to maintain his promises. The bloody sign of circumcision that prefigured the shedding of Christ's blood no longer remains appropriate after the Lamb of God has shed his blood once for all in order to remove our sin (cf. Heb. 10:10; 1 Peter 3:18). Therefore, New Testament believers receive a new sign for the covenant that indicates what Christ has accomplished for them. Baptism with water is the sign of the washing away of our sin (cf. Acts 22:16; 1 Cor. 6:11; Heb. 9:14).

Those who continue to demand circumcision as a requirement of God's covenant are condemned by the apostle,

who says, "For in Christ Jesus neither circumcision nor un-
circumcision has any value. The only thing that counts is faith
expressing itself through love" (Gal. 5:6). Circumcision no
longer remains a requirement for those who desire to obey
God (1 Cor. 7:18–19). Baptism is now the sign for all those who
desire to obey Christ and express their faith in him—men and
women, Jews and Gentiles (cf. Acts 2:38; 8:12; 10:47–48).

While the sign of the covenant changes, the features of
the covenant of faith do not. God continues to express his love
to those who have faith in him, and as a result all believers
share in the covenant that God prepared for Israel through
Abraham (Eph. 3:6). The promises continue to be extended
through parents to their children (Acts 2:38–39)—with the
ordinary condition remaining that these children must ulti-
mately express their own faith in Christ in order to reap the
full blessings of the covenant.

Emphasizing the continuity of the covenant as well as the
changed nature of the sign that accompanies it, the apostle
Paul writes to the Colossian believers, "In him [Christ] you
were also circumcised, in the putting off of the sinful nature,
not with a circumcision done by the hands of men but with the
circumcision done by Christ, having been buried with him in
baptism and raised with him through your faith in the power
of God, who raised him from the dead" (Col. 2:11–12). These
words remind us that salvation comes through faith, and also
that *the rite of circumcision that once signified the benefits of
Abraham's covenant has been replaced by baptism.*

Since the covenant remains but the sign changes, New
Testament believers would naturally expect to apply the new
sign of the covenant to themselves and their children as the
old sign was applied. Since the old sign was applied to children prior to their ability to express personal faith, there
would be no barrier to applying the new sign prior to a

child's personal profession of faith in Christ. Baptism would function as both a sign and a seal of the household's faith in Christ, just as the apostle Paul said (Rom. 4:11). As a sign, baptism would symbolize the washing away of sin for those who trusted in Christ's sacrifice for them. As a seal, baptism would indicate the visible pledge of God that when the conditions of his covenant were met, the promised blessings would apply.

THE BIBLICAL BASIS FOR INFANT BAPTISM

What evidence is there in the Bible that New Testament parents applied the sacrament of baptism to their children with the understanding that the covenant with Abraham remained in effect with a changed sign? Biblically minded Christians rightly want to see scriptural confirmation of their churches' practices. Thus, we who believe in infant baptism must confess that the lack of any specific example of infant baptism in the New Testament is a strong counterweight to our position. Conscientious Christians who object to infant baptism are not necessarily being superficial, ignorant, or mean-spirited. The church would not have argued the issues surrounding infant baptism for centuries if the right answers were obvious. What Presbyterians hope that believers will see in the absence of an example of a particular infant's being baptized is how strong the other biblical evidences must be to have kept this covenant practice dominant in the worldwide Christian church since the earliest centuries.

The Absence of a Contrary Command

Just as advocates of infant baptism must deal with the absence of an identified infant's being baptized in the New

Testament, so also must opponents of infant baptism face the absence of a specific command to deny children the covenant sign and seal. As has already been noted, the apostles took great care to emphasize the continuation of the Abrahamic covenant for New Testament believers. Throughout the two-thousand-year history of this covenant before the apostolic church began, the people of God had administered the covenant sign to their children. It seems highly probable that if the apostles had changed that practice, the change would have been recorded in the New Testament, either by example or by precept.

The removal of any sign of the covenant from believers' children would have been an immense change in practice and concept for Jewish families. After two thousand years of covenant-family practice (established since Genesis), a believing Jewish parent would not have known how to interpret a continuing Abrahamic covenant that did not administer the sign of the covenant to children. As will soon be discussed, the apostles frequently record that whole households are baptized after the head of the home believes in Christ. Consider how the head of a Jewish household would have reacted when others in the household (including servants and resident relatives) were baptized on the basis of his faith while his own children were denied the covenant sign.

The absence of a scriptural command to prohibit administering the sign of the covenant to children after two thousand years of observing such a practice weighs significantly against the view that the apostles wanted only those who were able to profess their faith to be baptized.

The Examples of Household Baptism

Further undermining the contention that only those who professed their faith were to be baptized are the examples of the apostles' expectations that entire households would be baptized once the head of the home accepted the gospel. Those who oppose infant baptism fairly ask for an example of an infant's being baptized in the New Testament. We have already acknowledged that there is no specific mention of an infant's baptism. But fairness requires that another question also be asked: Are there any examples of household members' being baptized because of the faith of the head of the household? Over and over again, the answer to this question is yes.

In fact, when we read the New Testament accounts of baptism, *every person identified as having a household present at his or her conversion also had the entire household baptized.* These accounts include every baptism of persons described in detail after the appointment of Christ's apostles (including Paul) was complete.

Household membership. Before listing these household baptisms, we should ask who were considered to be members of one's household in the ancient world. Returning to the Old Testament passages in which the covenant sign was first administered in households, we find that a household included all of one's resident dependents: spouse (if living), children (if present), resident relatives, and dependent servants not earning regular wages (e.g., Gen. 14:14–16; 17:23; Ex. 12:3–4). This understanding of households had governed Jewish thought and practice for two thousand years, and there is little reason to believe that the Scripture writers would have had any other perspective. There is no evidence that the New Testament writers used the concept of a household in a manner inconsistent with the common understanding of preceding centuries. No effort was made by the New Testament writers to indicate that children were no longer included in households—an exclusion that even today would be alien to our thought.

What is foreign to our thought today is the biblical principle of representative headship. Our lack of familiarity with this principle is one of the reasons why our individualistic culture finds it so difficult to accept the covenant-family principles and practices of Scripture. As has been discussed earlier, however, the presumption that the faith of the head of the home created obligations for the rest of the family was a historical understanding for God's people. Thus, when the Philippian jailer asked Paul, "What must I do to be saved?," it was natural and scriptural for the apostle to reply, "Believe in the Lord Jesus, and you will be saved—you and your household" (Acts 16:30–31). Paul's words do not mean that the rest of the household would automatically express genuine, saving faith in Christ, but his presumption was that the faith of the head of the household would govern the life and faith patterns of the rest of the man's family. As a result, the jailer's entire household was baptized that night (v. 33).

Household accounts. The account of the baptism of the Philippian jailer's household is particularly instructive because of the precise description supplied by Luke, the writer of Acts. Luke says that *all* of the jailer's household was baptized (v. 33), but then he uses a *singular* verb to describe who rejoiced and believed in God that night (v. 34). The jailer himself believed (singular verb), and his whole house was baptized. Sadly, this important distinction in the account is not reflected in some of our modern translations (see the English Standard Version for an excellent translation). As a result, some assume that entire households were baptized in the New Testament because everyone in them believed the gospel. While this is not impossible, it is unlikely that all those households consisted only of those who were old enough to make an intelligent faith commitment. Further, the assumption that everyone in those households must have made a faith commitment does not take notice of the careful distinction that Luke makes between those who actually believed and those who were baptized.

The other household baptisms recorded in the New Testament are well known: Cornelius and his household (Acts 10:47–48), Lydia and her household (Acts 16:15), and the household of Stephanas (1 Cor. 1:16). Crispus and his household should probably also be included in the list when one considers Acts 18:8 and 1 Corinthians 1:14 together.

The purpose for listing these accounts of household baptism is not to contend that individual adult believers were never baptized in the New Testament. Clearly, there were baptisms of individuals who apparently did not have households, such as Paul, the Ethiopian eunuch, and Simon the sorcerer (cf. Acts 8 and 9). Others were baptized during their pilgrimages or when household members apparently were not present (Acts 2:41; 19:5). There may also have been times when household members objected to being baptized. We do not know all the circumstances of the men and women who Scripture says were baptized (cf. Acts 8:12). What we do know is that when men and women believed in Christ, they were baptized. Further, whenever an individual baptism is described in detail in the New Testament, the members of the household, if they were present, also received the covenant sign of baptism.

Household resistance. The frequency of the household-baptism accounts demonstrates that it was normal and consistent with the ancient practice of the continuing Abrahamic covenant for heads of households to see that the covenant sign and seal were applied to all in their homes. No evidence indicates that children were excluded from these households.

Rather, two thousand years of covenant practice, combined with the absence of any command to exclude children, indicates that household baptisms included infants.

Infant baptism is sometimes resisted by people in North American culture today because they (1) do not understand the continuation of the covenant of faith made with Abraham and its application to all believers today, (2) are not informed of the representative nature of covenant headship, (3) do not understand how a covenant sign is a seal (i.e., that baptism is a visible pledge that covenant promises will apply when the conditions of faith are met, so that the sign does not have to be tied to the moment that one believes in Christ), (4) do not realize that children would have been included as members of households that were baptized, and (5) reject the idea of "dunking" a baby, if one's only experience with baptism involves immersion.

Immersion concerns. Of the issues causing resistance to infant baptism, only the issue of "dunking" babies has not been covered thus far. This booklet does not have space to deal comprehensively with the proper mode of baptism (sprinkling, pouring, or immersing), but I will briefly address the most common concerns. First, however, we should recognize that no preferred mode of baptism automatically rules out infant baptism. Some have assumed that if immersion is the only proper mode of baptism, then the Lord obviously does not intend for us to baptize infants. Yet there are major branches of Christianity in our world that do practice baptism by immersion and also baptize babies (quickly, I might add). Baptism by immersion does not rule out the possibility of infant baptism. But it should be acknowledged that most of the churches that practice infant baptism do not require baptism by immersion. Most of these churches teach that baptism is a ceremonial sign of Christ's cleansing and union with him, and that the amount of water used is not the key issue.

Ceremonial cleansing precedents. Various amounts of water are used in the ceremonial cleansings that Scripture describes with "baptism" language. In addition to examining the gospel narratives of Christ's baptism, we can discern the variety of ways that the Bible teaches baptism can be administered by looking at texts such as Mark 7:2–4 and Hebrews 9:10–22. English readers will be aided by knowing that the word often translated "washings" in these verses is the Greek word for *baptism*. These various ceremonial cleansings involve differing rites of pouring, dipping, and sprinkling. Tables (or "dining couches," ESV) and bowls were cleansed by "baptizing" them (see Mark 7:4). We readily understand of a bowl's being immersed, but a table would not be so easily "baptized" if immersion were the only type of cleansing in view. Also, in Jewish custom, water was poured over the hands for a ceremonial cleansing before eating, and the original language of the Bible refers to this practice as "baptizing" (see Luke 11:38).

The Hebrews passage mentioned in the preceding paragraph even refers to thousands of people being sprinkled at once (as well as their place of worship) with "baptism" language (cf. Ex. 24:6–8). I am not contending here that sprinkling is the only mode of baptism described in Scripture. As was mentioned previously, other Scriptures relate baptism to pouring such as when we are told of the pouring out of God's Spirit (cf. Luke 3:16; Acts 1:5; 2:17–18; Titus 3:5–6). The important point to note is not that there is only one proper mode of baptism, but rather that a baptism involves *a ceremonial cleansing in which the amount of liquid may vary according to the nature of the occasion.*

Adult baptism examples. Some people who have only at-
tended churches emphasizing the immersion of adults
upon a profession of faith may think that the Bible offers
conclusive evidence of how someone should be baptized in
its descriptions of adult baptisms. Yet the evidence is far
from conclusive. The accounts that say in certain English
translations that Jesus came "up out of the water" (Matt.
3:16; Mark 1:10) must be read in light of their times. Spig-
ots of running water were not common. To step down into
(or beside) a lake or river to obtain water for pouring or
sprinkling would be natural. A contextual reading of the
Greek could also say that Jesus came "away from" the water
after his baptism, without implying that he went into it.
And nowhere does the Bible say that Jesus (or anyone else)
went under the water for baptism. Philip baptized the
Ethiopian eunuch in a desert, where deep pools of water
would be unlikely. And the Bible tells us that the eunuch re-
quested baptism after reading from the portion of Isaiah
that says the Messiah will "sprinkle many nations" (Isa.
52:15; cf. Ezek. 36:25). Finally, the baptism of the Philippian jailer and his entire household occurred immediately
after a cataclysmic earthquake, when it seems unlikely that
they would have trailed through the town looking for a pool
of water after midnight (Acts 16:33).

The way in which the Bible presents the details of each
of the preceding adult baptisms makes it difficult to discern
the mode of baptism being used in each case—but this is a
blessing, not a problem. For those of us who see that a baptism is a ceremonial cleansing whose amount of liquid can
vary, the nonspecificity of details confirms our understanding. We live happily with this evidence that the mode of baptism could vary appropriately for the occasion, and note that
the Bible records numerous kinds of baptisms. Only those

who insist that baptism must be by immersion are forced to read the biblical details of adult baptisms in one particular way (in every case) that the descriptions of baptisms in other portions of Scripture do not require.

Apostolic analogies and infant implications. Some will say that the apostle Paul's language about being buried with Christ in baptism and raised again in newness of life (Rom. 6:4; Col. 2:12) clinches the case for immersion. But Presbyterians have noted through the centuries that the word translated "buried" relates more to the funeral ceremony than to the method of burial. Such an interpretation more closely coheres with Paul's argument in both passages, as he relates how we are united to Christ in baptism (see Rom. 6:3) because we have died with him to our old way of life and are now living with his indwelling resurrection power (see Rom. 6:5–11; Col. 2:11–13; 3:1–4). This perspective enables us to see why Paul so nearly compares circumcision and baptism (though they are very different things) because both identify us as being united to God and his people (cf. 1 Peter 3:21). This "identity" factor of baptism is less clear to us in a "Christian culture" today than it would have been to new believers in biblical times. Their baptisms clearly set them apart from their past, family, friends, and religion as they were united with other believers and their Lord in a new way of life.

Again, my goal here is not to prove that there is only one right way to baptize, but to address concerns about how the mode of baptism may affect our readiness to baptize our children. For parents who are concerned whether the mode of baptism determines whether they should baptize their child, the most important matter is not to clarify the details of every biblical account, but rather to note that a baptism is a ceremonial cleansing. The amount of water varied in the Bible, and the amount can vary today. A child can be truly baptized by sprinkling or pouring. Moms and dads do not have to worry about drowning their newborns in order to honor God's covenant.

THE BIBLICAL BENEFITS OF INFANT BAPTISM

Should we baptize infants because the sacrament will guarantee that our children will become genuine and eternal citizens of heaven? The answer is no, because no sacrament automatically creates or transmits the grace of salvation. The apostle Paul reminded the Corinthian Christians that although the ancient Israelites were all "baptized" by passing through the Red Sea under the cloud of God, many became idolaters who displeased God and experienced his wrath (1 Cor. 10:1–11). No mere ritual will save anyone.

But if baptism will not secure our children's eternity, then why should we administer the covenant sign and seal to them? The answer is that we baptize because God makes covenantal promises to believers and to their children. In baptism we honor God by marking out and acting on the promises that reflect his grace both in blessing parents who act in devotion to God and in blessing the child being devoted to him in covenantal faith.

The Devotion of Parents

Parents who love the Lord Jesus desire to devote all that they have to him. As Abraham devoted all that he had to God in the covenant of faith, so parents who trust in Christ want to demonstrate that their most precious gifts, their children, are his. In the sacrament of baptism, we as parents demonstrate our commitment to be faithful stewards of the precious gift of a child's soul that God grants us to nurture for a season of life.

Through the devotion that is demonstrated in baptism, parents begin to reap the blessings of obedience that come from building the foundations of a home on the promises of God. The baptism of an infant is the first public testimony of parents that they will trust and follow God in the raising of their child. As an act of devotion, the baptism sets the family on the path of blessing that God promises to those who walk in his ways.

The church witnessing the baptism is also blessed by the parents' testimony of devotion and trust. The church has the encouraging example of the parents' obedience, and fellow worshipers are reminded by the water of baptism that God's grace alone will wash away the sin of this child and fit him or her for heaven. In the salvation truths signified by the water of baptism, the parents humbly acknowledge that they are dependent on God's grace, not only to raise the child according to Scripture, but also to do what they themselves cannot do to make the child holy before God.

As a public act of devotion, baptism also makes the parents accountable to the church before which they take vows to raise their child in the nurture and admonition of the Lord. Accountability is not simply a willingness to accept advice and correction from others when things go wrong, but a humble and joyful desire to receive the spiritual resources of the church that will help a child grow in Christian character. In baptism, parents link the spiritual livelihood of their child to the spiritual life of the church. They promise to intertwine their family's life of faith with the life of the church so that they and the child will hear wise counsel from others (including more experienced parents), encounter the reality of God's presence in worship, and learn from the example of mature saints how God's grace forms the beauty of the soul in both good and difficult circumstances.

It is important to remember, however, that baptism is not merely a sign of God's grace—it is also a seal. Baptism does not simply signify what Christ has done, nor does it only demonstrate the parents' devotion. Baptism is also God's own continuing, visible pledge to his church that he will fulfill his covenant promises to those who place their faith in him. God is present in the sacrament as though the doors of heaven have opened for him to declare anew to his church, "By the marks of this sacrament, I promise that anyone who trusts in my mercy through the blood of Christ will have his sins washed away and will be as pure before me as the water that flows from this font, so that we will be in holy union forever." With this promise indicated by the seal of baptism, God reaches from heaven to embrace the parents and the child with the assurance of his grace, based on his mercy, not on their merit. In our moments of great pride in our children, and in our moments of great shame for our failings, *God's pledge of merciful grace that is evident in baptism is always ours by faith to claim* for ourselves and for our children.

The Blessing of the Children

The devotion of the parents who present their children for baptism places each child in a privileged position both to hear and to understand the truths of the gospel. The child first has the example of godly devotion demonstrated in the parents' willingness to devote their most precious possession to God. Beyond this initial example, the child lives in a home that through the child's baptism has promised to provide Christian nurture and to use the resources of the church to make that nurture truly biblical in character. The parents publicly promise in the sacrament of baptism to pray with and for their child, so that early in life the child might know the realities of God's saving grace in Christ.

The child also has the promise of the church to support the parents in his or her spiritual nurture and admonition. In the public sacrament of baptism, the people of the church vow to pray for the parents and the child, and to provide godly examples for them.

Some no doubt repeat these vows out of courtesy and convention, but as the church repeats its own testimony year after year, the whole body of Christ learns of its obligation and power to influence the eternity of her children. When the church is truly one in this effort, a child is surrounded and embraced by the testimony of Christ at every turn in life. Thus, the church becomes God's instrument of presenting the reality of Christ to the mind and heart of the child. A child with such an experience, fostered at baptism and nourished throughout his life by a mature body of believers, breathes the truths of grace as naturally and unconsciously as he or she breathes air.

In this atmosphere, faith naturally germinates and matures so that *it is possible, even common, for the children of Christian parents never to know a day that they do not believe that Jesus is their Savior and Lord.* Such covenantal growth of a child is, in fact, the normal Christian life that God intends for his people, and it is one of the most striking, but infrequently mentioned, reasons that baptism is rightly administered to infants.

Just as children are raised to know the color blue through those all about them who repeatedly and readily attest to the character of the hue, so children raised in an environment of faith ordinarily mature with an understanding of their Savior. Of course, there are exceptions. True faith remains a supernatural gift, but natural human instruments fulfilling their covenant obligations most frequently communicate it. Thus, as covenant children grow in natural understanding of their world, it is most common for them to mature with a parallel level of spiritual understanding. This means that it is no more likely that children nurtured in a consistently Christian home can specifically mark when they understood that Jesus was their Savior than they can mark when they knew that blue was blue.

Because of God's pattern of covenantal dealings with families, the ordinary path of baptized children of believing parents has a destination of genuine faith. For this reason such children also have the blessing of being treated as children of God by their parents. There is no reason to presume that because children are not yet able to express mature faith, they must be treated as unbelievers. It is not hypocritical to take them to church, urge them to express joy that Jesus loves them, or allow them to pray at bedtime, or make other such expressions of childish faith. To the contrary, it would be unbiblical to treat our children as offspring of Satan, unloved by God, and enemies of the household of faith, until they express saving faith. Such treatment that may be logically defensible, if one does not accept the covenant relation of a child to God, has no defense in Scripture (Ex. 12:25–27; Deut. 6:4–9; Eph. 6:4; Col. 3:21) or in the heart of any spiritually sensitive parent (Matt. 19:13–15; Luke 18:15–17). A child of believing parents has been baptized as a member of a believing household, is a child member of the body of Christ, and has been made holy by the representative faith of either or both parents. In years of maturity such children must still affirm personal faith, but long before such expressions are possible, Christian parents have the joy of treating their little ones as children loved by God who should be groomed for his glory—a joy that should privilege Christian children above all.

So when is the proper time to baptize such children? Since Genesis, the proper time that God declared for marking children with the covenant sign has been in their infancy in the covenant community. The early application of the sign indicated that there was not necessarily a definitive moment when a child made a life-altering decision to follow the Lord. Instead, children in believing homes were expected to grow in spiritual maturity and understanding as the covenant community embraced and instructed them. In a similar manner, the sacrament of baptism is rightly administered today to infants to indicate that their whole life is to be one of continually growing in Christ through the family that devotes them to God in faithfulness to the covenant they entered at birth.

The blessings of baptism that come upon parents and infants answer the common question: "Why not just wait?" To wait until a child proves that he or she is a Christian would deny the little one the early blessings of covenant baptism. In addition, if we really believed that we should not baptize persons until they proved they were Christians, then we would be forced to delay adult baptisms beyond the scriptural pattern also. When a child is baptized, God enters the scene. He promises to strengthen and enable the testimony and training of parents who seek his aid; he pledges to walk with—and fulfill covenant promises to—the child who matures in faith; and God uses the devotion of the parents and the church to further the spiritual nurture of the child. These covenant promises are too good to delay. The Scriptures that speak of them urge parents to share their blessings with their children at the earliest stages of life.

Words for Pastors

How should pastors explain the concept of infant baptism when administering the sacrament? The truths that underlie the practice are clear, but require an understanding of the scope of Scripture that many in our congregations lack today. As a result, many of the words of institution that are repeated during infant baptisms refer generally to God's love for his children or to Christ's willingness to allow children to approach him (e.g., Matt. 19:14; Luke 18:16). While such references accurately communicate the compassion of God, they are unconvincing as reasons for baptizing infants.

Those who disagree with infant baptism agree that Jesus said, "Let the little children come to me, and do not hinder them," and we are all aware that Jesus did not baptize the children who then approached him. Making the gospel accounts of Christ's blessing of children the chief emphasis of an explanation of infant baptism seems rather to prove that such ceremonies come more from sentiment and tradition than from any demonstrable biblical principle.

A number of fine books contain forms that help pastors frame credible words of explanation prior to an infant baptism. In addition, I have found the following words to be useful in my ministry:

> Will baptism save this child? No, salvation comes through trusting in Jesus Christ as one's Savior and Lord. Then why do we baptize this child? Not for sentiment, though he/she is sweet. Not for tradition, though it is dear. We baptize this child because we believe the Bible commands us to do so.
>
> Throughout biblical history, God promised to bless through a covenant relationship with his people. He said to Abraham, "I will be a God to you and to your children after you." Abraham believed God's covenant promise and devoted all that he had to the Lord, including the members of his household. In obedience

to God, Abraham showed his devotion through practicing the rite of circumcision in his household. This rite demonstrated that God's covenant would pass to future generations, but would necessitate the shedding of blood for sin.

The shed blood did not create the covenant, but rather acted as a seal, a pledge given by God, that he would honor his promise to all who, like Abraham, put their faith in him.

In the New Testament, the apostle Peter, preaching on the day of Pentecost, assured all that the covenant promises of God would continue for the children of believers. He said in Acts 2:38–39, "Repent and be baptized, every one of you, in the name of Jesus Christ for the forgiveness of your sins. . . . The promise is for you and your children and for all who are far off—for all whom the Lord our God will call."

The promise to bless through faith in God's grace continued, but the apostle Paul told the Colossian believers that the sign of this covenant had changed. No longer foreshadowing the shedding of Christ's blood, the New Testament sacrament of baptism is a sign of what Christ's blood accomplishes: the washing away of sin, and thus our union with him.

This water does not itself wash away sin, but rather, according to the apostle Paul, this sacrament acts as a seal—a visible pledge of God given to the church—whereby heaven assures us that when such children as this one express faith in Christ, all the promises of his covenant of grace will apply to them.

The Bible gives us good reason to express our covenant privileges through such a baptism. In the New

Testament accounts of baptism, every person identified as having a household present at his or her conversion also had the whole household baptized.

Yes, it is sweet to savor God's goodness to families, but sentiment is not what leads a church or parents to this holy ordinance. We baptize children in obedience to biblical teaching, in keeping with the precedent of centuries of faithful families, and in expectation of God's presence and blessing. God now uses this sacrament to pledge to us his faithfulness as we, in faith, devote this child of the covenant to him.